# From Anxious to Awesome

How to Transform Overwhelming and Negative Feelings into a Positive Guidance System That Can Lead You to Life You Want

By Alexcis Lopez

**MAKE THE MOST OF WHAT YOU LEARN AND
GET YOUR FREE BONUS**

CHECK OUT THE Free Worksheets AVAILABLE FOR YOU:
WWW.ANXIOUSTOAWESOME.COM

FROM ANXIOUS TO AWESOME
*HOW TO TRANSFORM OVERWHELMING AND NEGATIVE FEELINGS INTO A POSITIVE GUIDANCE SYSTEM THAT CAN LEAD YOU TO LIFE YOU WANT*

ALEXCIS LOPEZ

## LEGAL AND COPYRIGHT

Alexcis Lopez
transformativetouch@gmail.com

Limits of Liability and Disclaimer of Warranty
The author and publisher shall not be liable for your misuse of this material. This book is for strictly informational and educational purposes.

Ordering Information:
Quantity sales. Special discounts are available on quantity purchases by corporations, associations, and others. For details, contact the publisher at the address above.
Printed in the United States of America
First Edition
VERSION 1.2

## Dedication

THIS IS DEDICATED TO THE MANY CLIENTS WHO HAVE ENRICHED MY LIFE
SINCE I OPENED MY DOORS IN 2006
AND
TO MY BEAUTIFUL GODCHILDREN AND THE NEXT GENERATION —
TRUST YOUR FEELINGS, THEY WILL GUIDE YOU WHERE YOU NEED TO GO.

## Acknowledgements

Thank you to my husband Salvador who is always cheering me on. My family - mom who raised me and is always encouraging me to dream bigger, my dad and stepmom who share their support from Costa Rica, my in-laws who treat me like their own, and the sister of my heart and mother of my amazing god-children Christine. Without the love and support of my family I would not be able to fly so high or so far.

Thank you to my friend Pam who offered me the invitation that actually got me to finally start writing the book. To Mike and Ed and the You Everywhere Now team. To the Op Ed Project and the mentors who work so tirelessly to help women own their voices. To my fantastic editor Rob who made the process so much easier.

To my teacher and mentors along the way - Michael Bennett, Cal Banyan, Don Alberto, Rick Oliver, Barry Schimmel, Abraham Hicks and to the many unseen guides - you know who you are - Thank you!

And finally, to all my extended family, friends and clients, too many to name, that have been a part of my story, thank you all for your love and support.

# TABLE OF CONTENTS

# A VISION

*"Always listen to your heart." – my mom*

In December 2007, my search to answer the mysteries of feelings led me to the jungles of Peru. I was about to take part in an Ayahausca ceremony led by Don Alberto, a native shaman. Ayahausca, a visionary medicine, had been used for healing in the Amazon for a millennia. I hoped that it could help me untangle some of my own feelings and in the process, help me to understand more about feelings in general. There I was, in a hut, in the middle of the jungle, with no electricity. I was drinking a concoction described as "liquid spirit" made of vines, leaves and bark collected earlier in the day, to see if I could journey into the dark night of my soul and come out a bit wiser on the other side.

As the visionary brew took effect, I awoke to an inner hell. I was drowning in a sea of anger, sadness, fear, shame and pain that had haunted me since my childhood. I couldn't get away from the feelings, no matter how hard I resisted. I couldn't get a moment's rest to think or take a breath. There was no way out, and time had fallen away. How long had I been there in that hell of feelings? How many lifetimes had I spent thrashing around trying to fight my way free? The experience went on and on until I was sure I couldn't take any more, and then it went on some more.

Finally, exhausted to my very core, with no idea how long I had been trapped inside myself, I cried out to whoever would listen. "Why?" I asked. "Why can't I just be free? How do I get rid of these bad feelings?" From over my right shoulder, as if it had only been waiting for me to ask, a calm voice replied, "There are no bad or good feelings. It is you that judges them as bad or good. The feelings are only guideposts meant to lead the way. Stop fighting them. They are messengers and cannot leave until you receive the message. Turn toward the feelings as allies, and you will find what you seek."

As the voice spoke, the sea of feelings inside me calmed, and I floated looking up at a sky so full of stars it took my breath away. Could the voice be right, I wondered? Had I been misinterpreting the role of feelings my entire life? Did I have enough courage to turn toward myself and all that I was feeling? Did I really have any other choice?

I watched the stars for a timeless moment, aware of the dark waters that I floated upon, of the unknown depths of my feelings waiting to swallow me whole. "Ok," I said to the voice, to myself, to the star-laden Universe, "let's do this." I let my feelings in, sank gently into the sea of my vision, opened myself to the messages they had been trying to tell me, and everything shifted.

***

When I started my coaching and bodywork practice in 2006, I quickly realized that unresolved feelings were the first cause for much of the mental, emotional and physical disease that my clients experienced. This sparked a series of questions for me that at the time I had no answers for:

- How is it that we can be born with feelings and live with them our entire lives and yet they seem to be a complete mystery to us?
- How could we not have answers to the fundamental what, where and why of feelings?
- Is there a better way to be working with our feelings?
- What exactly are the purpose of feelings?

Seeking the answers to these questions would guide and shape my journey, personally and professionally, over the next decade. I would complete a Master's in Science in Metaphysics, become certified in Clinical Hypnotherapy, Neuro-Linguistic Programming, Life Coaching and a multitude of different Energy and Body healing modalities all in search of the "why" of feelings.

When I started my journey, I had a lot of my own unresolved feelings that seemed to be keeping me stuck. I believed many of the myths about feelings:

✓ There are bad feelings
✓ Feelings lie
✓ Feelings are foolish
✓ Listen to your head not your heart
✓ Feelings are weak
✓ Feeling are a woman's thing
✓ Feelings get in the way

What I discovered in my journey was the complete opposite. Feelings *aren't in the way* of what we want, they are *showing us the way* to what we want. Like an inborn GPS, once understood in their proper role, feelings are our guides to creating the life we were born to live.

What I offer on these pages is the 101 guidebook on how

to transform your relationship with your feelings so you stop working against and start working with your feelings. The transformational journey from negative feelings to a life filled with peace, trust, joy, empowerment, abundance and connection begins when we decide that *what we feel actually matters*! When you finish this book, you will be able to:

- ✓ Answer the where, what and why of feelings
- ✓ Correctly interpret the messages feelings bring
- ✓ Have appropriate and healthy actions to choose from to aid you in addressing the messages you receive
- ✓ Understand yourself better
- ✓ Will have resources to turn to that will help support your well-being

This book marks the beginning of a journey of self-discovery. The life you want is waiting, and your feelings are going to help you get there. Let's get started!

# CHAPTER 1
# FEELINGS EXPLAINED IN A NUTSHELL

*"Negative emotion is your best friend, because it is telling you in the moment, that you are headed in opposition to what you want..." – Abraham-Hicks*

Our journey to understanding feelings starts with our unconscious mind, which is where feelings originate. The unconscious, by its very nature, is outside of our conscious control and therefore a subject of great uncertainty and distrust.

A great deal more is controlled by the unconscious than most people know – survival protocols, autonomic body functions, beliefs, habits, long term memories, dreams, imagination, needs, feelings and more. While the conscious mind is logical, linear and able to judge the information it is given, its weakness is the limited amount of information that it can process or hold at any given moment. The unconscious, on the other hand, has extraordinary power to process and store information, which is why it is responsible for our long-term memories, habits and beliefs. Creative and timeless, the unconscious always works in the present. These two minds complement each other when used together as they were meant to be. The unconscious needs the conscious mind's ability for critical thinking while the conscious needs the unconscious mind's unlimited power and creativity. To work together, there must be a way for these minds to communicate and feelings are the answer.

### The Purpose of Feelings

Fundamentally, feelings are an energetic form of language that our unconscious mind uses to communicate with our conscious mind. Feelings give information to the conscious mind about our state of being. In other words, feelings tell us about our overall condition (mind, body and spirit) and whether we have what we need to experience an optimal state of being or not.

Naturally, our state of being is one of well-being with ourselves and the world at large – as long as our needs are met. Feelings arise when we have fallen out of sync with our natural state due to a need, that once addressed, allows us to return to our natural state of well-being once again. Feelings and needs are interdependent – the one, feelings, giving information about the other, needs.

The No. 1 directive of our unconscious self is to ensure that our needs are met so that we can survive and therefore have the opportunity to prosper. To this end, it's as if we have an inborn GPS that is programmed when we are born by our unconscious mind to seek out positive states of well-being in which we thrive – happiness, peace, joy, connection, respect, empowerment, acceptance and so on. We know when we have not reached these positive states when we experience negative feelings. In this way, feelings are the part of the GPS that gives us course corrections. Feelings alert us to the fact that we have taken a wrong turn and then tell us, by which specific feeling(s) is used, what needs must be addressed to bring us back on course.

Once we understand that feelings are a guidance system, it clears up a few general misconceptions we have:

- ✓ Feelings aren't bad or good, only energetic information. Feelings alert us to the experience of an unmet need, which by its very nature is a negative experience, but neither the need(s) nor the feeling(s) themselves are bad.
- ✓ There is no right or wrong to feelings and needs. We have a right to feel what we feel and to need what we need. No one can nor should tell us how to feel or what to need.
- ✓ Feelings aren't logical. As a tool of the unconscious mind, feelings are not based on logical or linear thinking. That is not to say that feelings don't make sense, just that they don't follow the same criteria as logic. Just because they aren't logical doesn't mean that they aren't important.
- ✓ As part of the unconscious, feelings always work in the present. We don't actually suffer from past feelings, only present feelings. While the event that caused the feelings may be in the past, the unresolved feeling themselves stay current until they are addressed.
- ✓ Feelings don't define us. While feelings have vital information about our state of being, and may color our perspective they are fleeting experiences and are not who we are in any permanent sense.

Read the above statements a few times. Understanding the true nature of feelings is the foundation for any future transformational work that we do with them. There must be a fundamental change in the way that we think about feelings and in extension our unconscious selves. The unconscious is an important part of *who we are*. Through years of working with the unconscious, I can say with 100% conviction that our unconscious selves want to work with us to create the life we consciously want. Remember that it was our unconscious that programmed our GPS with those positive states in the first place.

The key to living the life we want is to learn to work with our feelings, connecting our two minds, and getting us back on course to well-being.

# CHAPTER 2
# PRIMARY FEELINGS

*"The more you hide your feelings, the more they show.*
*The more you deny your feelings, the more they grow."*
*– Unknown*

There are a few different schools of thoughts about how many basic or primary feelings we have, but it usually falls between four and eight. A colleague and mentor, Rick Oliver, a psychologist and inner child therapist, uses seven primary feelings in his own work, and after studying with him I began using the same because it was simple and effective.

The seven primary feelings are *Anger, Fear, Joy, Loneliness, Pain, Sadness* and *Shame*. Like primary and secondary colors on a color wheel, the primary feelings can stand on their own or be combined to create a variety of other feelings.

These seven primary feelings will be our focus during the next few chapters. Each feeling is connected to a different need. Everything we need to know is carried in the message of the feeling when we understand the language. We know, by which feeling is sent, which need is unmet and what we need to do to self-correct and get back on course to well-being. See the next page for a list of those seven primary feelings.

As we get ready in the next chapter to work with our

primary feelings, here are some guidelines to keep in mind:

| Feeling | Need | State of Being Experienced when Need Is Met |
|---------|------|---------------------------------------------|
| Anger | Need Protection/Respect/Fairness | Peaceful/Respected/Empowered |
| Fear | Need Safety | Trust/Content/Safe |
| Joy | Need to receive, allow & share | Appreciation/Ease/Joy/Abundance |
| Lonely | Need Connection | Connection/Belonging |
| Pain | Need to pay attention! | Wellness/Awareness |
| Sad | Need to Let Go/Grieve | Acceptance |
| Shame | Need to know self-worth | Empowerment/Confidence/Worthiness |

## Always Bring It Back to The Primary Feelings

We use a lot of descriptive words to describe the primary feelings. Take anger, for example. Think of how many different words we use to describe our level of anger – irritated, cross, protective, provoked, incensed, bitter, resentful, ticked off, pissed, annoyed, upset, hateful, hostile, enraged, aggressive, to name just a few.

We even use the same word sometimes to describe different primary feelings. For example, "desolate" could describe a feeling of pain, sadness, loneliness or a mix of all of them. In the end, we must decide which primary feeling(s) we are describing at any given moment depending on our own experience.

These descriptive words are to primary feelings as shades of a color are to the original color. When we work with feelings, we always use the primary feeling no matter what level of that feeling we are experiencing. Whether we are slightly annoyed or downright enraged, we are still dealing with anger and the need for protection, respect and/or fairness. While the intensity of the need may vary, the need is still of the same theme.

## We Can Feel More Than One

We often experience more than one feeling at a time, and we can combine two or more primary feelings to create mixed feelings. When working with mixed feelings, we need to take the time to figure out each primary feeling we are experiencing. Take jealousy for example. In one case, when we feel jealousy, it may be mainly made of anger, with some pain and sadness. In another instance, jealousy could be mainly shame with loneliness, fear and anger. We would identify what we feel as jealousy both times, yet the mix is different, and for that reason how we need to respond will differ as well. That's why untangling what we are feeling down to the primary feeling(s) is so important.

## We Pick Up on Other People's Feelings

We can feel other people's feelings to varying degrees depending on our sensitivity and how intimately we know the person. Feelings are energy, and energy can be transferred. Doing a self-check to see if we might be allowing someone else's feeling to either cloud or accentuate ours is always a good idea. Just ask yourself – is there any part of what I am feeling that may be someone else's? Whatever your first impression is – yes or no – go with it. Those first impression, gut reactions or "knowings" that we receive are the unconscious mind speaking to us. Too often we discount the information that comes to us from the unconscious because the way the information comes seems illogical. Have you ever met someone and disliked them right off the bat for no apparent reason? Usually we talk ourselves out of our first instinct because it seems silly or unreasonable. How can we dislike someone we don't even know? I have done this plenty of times, ignored the subtle warnings of my unconscious only to regret it later when I find out that the person is dishonest or that they are the type that uses people. The moral of the story is start paying more attention to your first impressions. If your impression is that you are being influenced by another person's feelings, then ask that whatever isn't yours be released. You can even imagine a colored energy leaving your body, if that helps. This may sound weird or "woo-woo," yet it works. If you have been carrying a lot of other people's feelings from past events, then you may need to do this "releasing" multiple times as more of it comes up. If you are sensitive to picking up energy in general, then making this a daily practice can be very helpful in keeping you clearer and more centered in your own experience.

**Feelings vs. Emotions**

You may wonder why I keep talking about "feelings" instead of "emotions." In general, we use these words interchangeably, but they are not strictly the same, and understanding the difference can be quite enlightening.

Feelings are the *unconscious experience* of internal stimuli, physical and mental in nature. When we are in danger, for example, our unconscious mind almost instantaneously processes the external information and triggers the physical fight-or-flight response – increasing heart rate, blood flow, respiration and releasing adrenaline – all to aid us in escaping the danger. In the case of a bear chasing us, this process is a lifesaver, and we may not even really feel the fear until we have safely escaped the situation. Once safe, we have time for our unconscious to interpret the stimuli we just experienced as fear. Consider, however, that we experience the same physical and chemical changes in less life-threatening situations like public speaking when we have plenty of time to feel the unconscious experience of all that stimuli as fear in the moment. Ironically, this can make public speaking more frightening to most people than being chased by a bear.

Emotions are the *conscious expression* of the unconscious feeling. Although many of us use our feelings as an excuse for bad behavior ("It was the anger that made me do it."), the truth is that we are all responsible for how we *choose to express* what we are feeling. Being angry and not yelling, even though we may want to, is a good example of how we can choose how to express what we are feeling.

**States of Being**

Since states of Being are at the center of our feelings and needs, let's be clear about how they affect us. There are both negative and positive states of Being. Incorporating the condition of our physical, mental and spiritual states, our state of Being gives rise to our attitude(s), moods, expectations, beliefs and patterns of interaction with others. Like a framework upon which our experience of life is built, states of Being are stable so long as we continue to meet the conditions needed to perpetuate the state(s).

When we ignore, deny or hold onto a feeling, we then find ourselves experiencing negative states of suffering such as depression, anxiety, despair, resentment, stress and worthlessness.

When we listen to our feelings and course correct by addressing the needs that are brought to our attention, we experience positive states such as worthiness, empowerment, happiness and hope.

The conditions needed to maintain a positive state of Being change from person to person and from situation to situation, which is why there needs to be a tool (feelings) for our unconscious mind to communicate what is needed in any given moment.

# CHAPTER 3
# UNPACKING FEELINGS

*"We think too much and feel too little." – Charlie Chaplin*

There is a general process to "unpacking a feeling," that we will be following in subsequent chapters, as we explore each of the primary feelings. Unpacking our feelings is the process that helps us to figure out the why, who, how much and what next when we experience a feeling. This process is the "how" of transforming our experience of negative feelings into a course correction by shifting our focus from the feeling (the messenger), to the need (the message), to the repair which is the how we make lasting change.

Here is an overview of the process that will be applied to each of the seven primary feelings:

• **Identify the feeling**: By naming what we feel, we shift the experience from the unconscious into the conscious. There are times when just acknowledging a feeling is all that will be needed, and in those cases the feelings will dissipate once we name it. In most cases, though, it is the first step of the unpacking process.

• **Identify the Need**: A feeling points to a need. Acknowledging the need begins to shift our focus from the feeling, which is just the messenger to the message itself of an unmet need. Knowing which specific need(s) the primary feeling is connected to is crucial to our ability to take action in a positive and healthy manner.

• **Identify the Cause**: This is where we observe and discern what brought about the feeling to help us further understand the need and to gather information so we can make a better decision about what action(s) may be required to address the need. We can ask:

a) Is the cause external? When the cause of our feeling is external versus internal there will be different actions called for.

b) Is the cause internal? Internal causes are often the most complex. This is when the unpacking process really goes to work.

c) Mistakes are made when we treat an external threat like an internal threat or visa-versa.

• **Self-Reflection**: Once we have named the feeling, need and cause, the time arrives to ask ourselves some questions that will deepen our understanding of our experience and help us decide what types of actions may be appropriate.

• **Time for Action**: Having reflected upon what we have unpacked, next comes the time to take action. We always start with ourselves first and then move outward:

a) Internal Actions: These are actions we can do inside ourselves or for ourselves.

b) External Actions: These are actions that we take with other people.

There will be specific actions given for particular feelings, but a few general actions that can be used for any feeling:

✓**Exercise and Nutrition**: Remember that feelings alert us to **any** unmet need – mental, physical or spiritual. Our physical state is an important part of our overall well-being. We may feel angry, fearful, sadness or pain if we are not getting enough exercise, sleep or the right nutrition. Since feelings are energy, exercise can be very beneficial in relieving excess energy so that we can think more clearly and be more centered. Nutritionally, food allergies have been shown, sometimes, to cause anxiety and depression, while natural foods, vitamins and oils have proven effective for treating anxiety, depression and grief, even outperforming medications in comes cases. Taking the time to research ways in which you could better support your health always marks an excellent and appropriate action.

✓**Gratitude:** Time and again, a practice of gratitude has been shown to help support states of well-being. This is because gratitude helps us to focus our attention on what is working for us. Optimally, we start and end our day in gratitude and appreciation.

✓**Meditation**: Spending 15-20 minutes of quiet time is an important ingredient in building and growing our relationship with ourselves. This time helps the conscious and the unconscious to integrate and communicate. An easy way to meditate is to find a quiet space where you will not be interrupted. Set a timer for 15 minutes. Sit with your feet on the floor and your back as straight as you can manage (use a pillow to help prop you up). Close your eyes and breathe. Follow your breath. Don't try to not think.

That usually doesn't work. Let your thoughts come and go as you focus on your breath. If you find yourself following your thoughts just bring yourself back to your breath. Be aware of what you feel. It's as easy and challenging as that. Being uncomfortable, bored or fidgety in the beginning is natural and means you are onto something. Just keep showing up every day and invest 15 minutes to quiet time with yourself and your breathing, and you will begin to see returns mentally and physically.

✓**Own Your Influences:** We are ultimately responsible for what we allow to influence us externally. Take control and be picky about who you spend your time with, and what you watch, read and listen to. My dad told me, "Show me who you spend time with, and I will tell you who are." Over time, I have come to see the wisdom in his words. Choose to be around positive, uplifting, inspirational and abundance-minded people. This may sound harsh, but spending time with people who are negative, scarcity minded, depressive and complaining sorts doesn't help you and doesn't help them. Reading, watching or listening to negative influences is just as damaging. If you want to live in states of well-being, then support states of well-being by taking charge of the influences you allow in your environment.

✓**Own your head-space**: There are two parts to owning your head-space – beliefs and self-talk. Many of our beliefs were introduced to us at such a young age we don't even remember how they came to be. This is dangerous because we take those early beliefs for granted, never stopping to question them. Beliefs have a lot to do with feelings. If, for example, we believe that "life is hard, I have to fight for every little thing" our belief is not in alignment with a state of well-being. Repeat it to yourself again and see how you feel as you say it – *"Life is hard, and I must fight for every little thing."* I feel fear first, then some sadness and then anger. What do you feel?

Those feelings tell me that this belief is going to lead me away from where I want to be – away from states of peace, abundance, ease, trust and safety. Start questioning your beliefs, to see how they make you feel, and to change them if they don't feel good. When changing beliefs, we must replace them with better beliefs. The unconscious mind works best when it is given another belief to exchange for the outdated one. So I might change the above belief into "Life can be easy and I am open to receiving abundance daily."

Beliefs lead into the second part of our head space which is self-talk. We all talk to ourselves; the important question to ask is *Do you know what you are telling yourself?* If we believe that "life is hard, and I have to fight to get anything I need," then our self-talk will probably be fearful and angry. One of the most vital resources we can practice is soothing self-talk. Learning to say kind, comforting, positive and uplifting thoughts to ourselves is amazingly healing.

Be patient as you make these changes. It takes time to shift beliefs and thoughts that we have been feeding for decades. By replacing our beliefs and self-talk with better feeling thoughts, we lay the foundation for healthier, happier states of Being.

✓ **Journaling:** Writing is a great way to gain distance and perspective. Whether you are writing a list to help you stay on track and remember action items or you're detailing your feeling, needs and thoughts, writing allows you to "see" what is in your mind. You may be surprised by what you find. Once you've put your "mind on paper" then you will have a better idea of what needs your attention.

✓ **Ask yourself what you are feeling:** Caring about how you feel is important. Take time throughout the day to ask yourself how you are feeling and listen to the answer. If you are feeling something and don't have time to unpack it in that moment, you can set it aside, as long as you make a plan to come back to it in a timely manner.

✓ **Ask for help**: We can isolate ourselves because we don't want to be a burden, or we don't want others to see our vulnerability. We all go through challenging times in our lives, and there will be times when all of us will need help whether it's just the ear of a friend or more professional aid. The thing to remember is that you are not alone. There are many options; from family to professionals to group therapy to support groups online. If you are struggling, you don't have to go it alone. Please ask for help, you are worth it.

We will see this entire unpacking process and these general actions again in each chapter along with more specific information for each primary feeling. Take note that 80% of the unpacking process is about us getting clear and taking responsibility for ourselves before we ever engage the outside world. This means that, unless it is a clear external threat that we must fight, flee or hide from, we do not react first but take time to decide the best course of action after much introspection. Also remember that the questions and actions asked in each chapter are jumping off points. As you become more familiar with this unpacking process you will organically begin to find other questions and actions that are appropriate for your unique experience.

# CHAPTER 4
# ANGER

### Honoring Our Boundaries

*"Anybody can become angry – that is easy, but to be angry with the right person and to the right degree and at the right time and for the right purpose, and in the right way...that is not easy." – Aristotle*

Jack's hands tightened into fists, as he stared at the online credit card statement. He had just told his wife, again, last week, that they needed to stick to their budget, and she had gone right out and spent more than $400. Jack closed his eyes in deep frustration and exhaled forcefully trying to calm his growing anger. It is obvious that his wife didn't take him or their financial situation seriously.

Sally sighed and rubbed her temples, as she contemplated her desk and the numerous folders of work still waiting for her attention. Most of the work wasn't even hers. Somehow, she ended up taking on tasks that actually belonged to her colleagues. As she silently asked herself why she couldn't ever seem to say no, Jan from accounting popped her head in. "Hey Sally. I was wondering if you could send out some email for me regarding some accounts receivables. I would do it, but you are just so much better at it than I am. I really appreciate it. Thanks!" Jan is gone before Sally had time to utter a word and there is now one more folder on her desk. Sally feels an uncomfortable feeling in her chest that she is afraid to name, and a throbbing began in her head.

The Shaman's dark eyes sparkled, as he smiled kindly at me. "You have undigested anger in your belly that is making you sick." Since childhood, my digestion had been an issue. For many years, I struggled with stomach pain and bloating. Conventional medicine had not turned up any satisfying answers. I wasn't interested in medicating myself, and my gut (pun intended) told me there was an emotional core to my dis-ease. I started seeking answers in alternative medicine – energy therapies, bodywork, healers. That led me to the small house in rural Arizona where I sat. The healer, introduced to me as "Grandfather," laid his callused hands gently upon my belly, then my heart, and then my brow quietly meditating. "Anger is like a machete," the healer continued in his soft, melodic voice. "It can protect us, clear a path in the jungle, cut food, and it can hurt and kill. It can be used for much good, much that is important, but when we don't learn it's right use, we slash everything, us too. You are afraid of the machete, so you hold it tight, so tight it is cutting you instead of protecting you. Time to learn how to use your machete."

Anger is the fight half of the fight-or-flight response and a vital part of our unconscious survival mechanisms. Anger speaks to the primal need to protect and demand respect for our bodies, property, time, needs or any person, place or cause that we think of as important to us. At its core, anger is an agent for change, a call to take positive action by standing up for ourselves, fighting for what we believe is fair or asking for what we need. When used appropriately, anger is a transformational force; misuse of it, however, can be extremely harmful to ourselves and others.

When we think anger, think boundaries. Boundaries create protection while also defining conduct. Take the need for respect in a relationship for example. For couples, one way this need for respect may be translated into a boundary would be around an expectation of monogamy. Should that boundary be broken, the natural result will be feelings of anger. Clear boundaries help other people to know what we need, how best to interact with us, and what will and won't be allowed. Unclear or missing boundaries can lead to a variety of misunderstandings and dysfunctional interactions in which we get hurt or end up hurting others. Beyond the more obvious boundary violations, such as being robbed or physically assaulted, there are many subtle boundaries that are crossed everyday – someone takes advantage of us, a colleague spreads gossip about us, a friend tries to pressure us into something we don't want to do, a client constantly disrespects our time. Anger is a vital alarm system that when appropriately honored creates opportunities to experience clarity, growth, respect, peace and empowerment.

## Anger Gone Wrong

If, on the other hand, we don't understand anger's message, then there are many ways in which to misuse or avoid anger. Here are two common examples of dysfunctional angry behavior.

**Exploder:**

The exploder is the type of behavior that gives anger its bad reputation. Exploders plug into the temporary power and energy that anger offers. Fundamentally disrespectful of others, the Exploder does not take responsibility for themselves or their actions by using their feelings of anger as an excuse for their behavior. Even when there is good reason for the anger, exploding on others verbally or physically is neither an appropriate nor an effective way to respond to the need for better boundaries that anger alerts us to.

This explosive behavior is learned in childhood either by being a victim of an explosive parent's abuse or by discovering the power of childhood tantrums in getting them what they wanted. While Exploders can be both men and women, anger is generally perceived as a more "manly" feeling. Due to this, anger can be a "safer" feeling for many men to express instead of the "weaker" feelings of pain, sadness, loneliness or fear. In this way, an Exploder's anger is often a smokescreen for other feelings that they are not allowing themselves to feel.

**Imploder:**

In contrast to the Exploder, anger for the Imploder is the forbidden feeling. Their way of dealing with anger is the equivalent of plugging their ears and employing the "la-la-la" technique. They stuff, swallow, and ignore their anger, which means it has to find some other ways of expressing itself such as physical symptoms of headaches or, in my case, digestive issues.

Imploders were often punished in childhood for standing up for themselves or had very dominant parents. They may have been abused by or witnessed the rages of an explosive parent, which only cemented the idea that anger is uncontrollable and something to fear. The Imploder is overly sensitive about hurting someone else's feelings or losing someone they care for should they show any anger. The Imploder also may have received the message that they aren't worthy of protection or were not allowed to protect themselves. Without healthy boundaries and fearful of confrontation, the Imploder plays the part of the human "doormat" and tends to feel used and abused by the world around them.

We need to observe our own relationship with anger. Do we feed it or fear it? Do we use it as an excuse for bad behavior or let others walk over us because we are too afraid to stand up for ourselves? What did we learn about anger from our families? Knowing our own tendencies will help us to work with and heal our relationship with anger.

## Unpacking Anger

As Aristotle so wisely put it, we must make sure that we are "angry with the right person and to the right degree and at the right time and for the right purpose, and in the right way." Whenever we unpack a feeling, we are working out the right who, why, and what.

Time to unpack our first primary feeling and see this process in action.

**Identify the Feeling**: First we must identify the feeling. If you would describe what you are feeling with any of these words than you may be working with anger – *irritated, protective, enraged, hateful, hostile, sore, pissed, annoyed, upset, offended, bitter, resentful, aggressive, infuriated, incensed, cross, boiling, seeing red, indignant, fuming, seething, rebellious, explosive, inflamed, provoked, unpleasant, ticked off, frustrated.*

**Identify the Need**: We have identified that we are feeling angry which means there is an unmet need around boundaries, protection and/or fairness.

**Identify Cause:** What type of boundary violation are we dealing with? With anger, there are two categories of boundary violation – extraordinary and ordinary violations.

**Extraordinary Violation:** Are we in a *life-threatening* and *immediate danger* from which we need to fight to protect ourselves or another person's life? Examples would be a gun to our head, someone trying to overpower or attack us.

**Immediate Action:** In these cases, there is no time for drawn out thinking, we need to fight with everything we have to survive. A life or death situation in which we are defending ourselves or another person is *the one time when we have a right to use all that angry energy at full force* to protect ourselves. Once we are in a protected position and safe, then we can decide if there is further action or proactive actions needed to keep us protected in future. If you are not in a life-threatening situation, then there is no reason or excuse to use anger to physically attack or overpower another person.

**Ordinary Violation:** When dealing with ordinary boundary violations, we have time to consider a variety of responses. This is where the work really begins. Before any action can be taken we must know what boundary was crossed and by whom. It's a bit like playing the board game Clue where we need to know which person was in which room with which object before we can solve the crime or in the case of anger know best how to respond. Some examples of ordinary violations where the person and the violation has been identified include: the co-worker who keeps eating our food at work even when it is clearly labeled; a parent who tells strangers inappropriate and intimate information about our lives without our consent; the client who consistently doesn't pay their bill in a timely manner; the stranger who pushes in front of us in line; the friend who never hears "no" for an answer.

Note that if we are not sure what triggered our anger, then it is important that we take the time to investigate before taking any action.

**Self-reflection – questions to ask yourself:**
- Is my anger hiding another feeling that I am not comfortable facing?
- Is this anger really about this situation? Or am I not getting what I need and therefore find myself in a "bad" or irritable mood (consider sleep, exercise, being unwell or any number of other factors that can leave us overly sensitive to what would otherwise be a normal experience)?
- Do I need to take better care of myself in some way?
- Am I angry at this particular person/situation or am I taking my anger out on them instead of dealing with what/who is really bothering me?

- Is the amount of anger I am feeling proportionate to the offense? If it seems excessive then what else is bothering me?
- Is this a situation in which I need to involve another person or is this something that I can take care of myself?
- Have I been clear about the boundary that was violated? Did I clearly communicate the boundary to the person or did I just assume that they should know that I had a boundary about this issue?
- Am I feeling any anger that isn't mine?
- Am I using all the resources at my disposal?

**Taking Action**

Once we know that we have identified the cause and have clarified further with our self-reflection it is time to start taking any actions that will help address the need. Remember that we always start with ourselves first before taking any external actions.

**Internal Action(s):**

✓ Take care of an unmet need for yourself: If you can remedy an unmet need yourself, all the better. Learning to take care of your needs is very empowering.

✓ Take better care of yourself: Get regular exercise. Prioritize sleep and nutrition. If you think that there is a food component then seek out a doctor's help in testing for food allergies.

✓ Meditate 15 minutes a day: Meditation and mindfulness practice help us to stay centered and less affected by outside conditions.

✓Give yourself permission to care about how you feel! Limit or eliminate angry influences. For many of us there are particular people or things that push our angry button. Take watching the news, for example; if you get angry every time you watch the news, that isn't a good thing. You are responsible for what you allow to affect you, so either manage the amount of time that you engage with such triggers or cut them out completely.

✓If you realize that your anger is hiding another feeling, then do the work to unpack that other feeling.

✓If you realize that you're using the present situation as a scapegoat for the real reason you're angry, refocus your anger on what is truly bothering you and ask further questions as to why you were looking for scapegoats in the first place.

✓Take time to make sure that you are very certain about your boundaries in the particular circumstance you find yourself in. If you are not clear, then you will not be able to clearly communicate it to someone else.

✓Release any anger that is not yours.

✓Question and replace angry beliefs with new beliefs about how protected you are, how you are empowered to create healthy boundaries, how you can get what you need with ease and about how life can be peaceful.

✓Use soothing self-talk. Too often when we are

angry, we dwell and seethe in our minds – "I can't believe that they did that! How dare they! Who do they think they are!" Instead focus on the positive lessons you've learned from the experience and how you will do things differently next time. "Wow, that really made me angry. I am so glad that I have this opportunity to get clearer on my boundaries. Next time I will be that much better at standing up for myself. The clearer I get about what I will allow in my life the healthier relationships I will foster. I am really grateful to my feelings for bringing these needs to my attention."

✓ Practice gratitude.

✓ If the person who violated your boundaries is a repeat offender, you have a choice to make. You do not have control over them. You cannot make them respect your boundaries. If you have repeatedly asked and they have repeatedly ignored you, then you can either:

   1. Cut off relations with them.
   2. If they are someone you still want to have in your life (a parent or sibling who does not respect your boundaries for example), then you must own the choice that you are remaining connected without any expectation that they will change and respect your boundaries. This relationship may not ever be particularly healthy, but by owning your choice, taking responsibility for your actions and managing

your time around them you can have a better experience.

**External Action(s):**

✓ Have a conversation to clarify and agree upon a boundary.

✓ Have a conversation to enforce or give a warning about a boundary that has already been communicated and agreed upon.

✓ Remove yourself from an unwanted negative or angry situations or influence.

✓ Cut off a relationship with someone who has repeatedly disrespected clearly stated and agreed upon boundaries.

✓ Ask someone else if they are willing and able to meet a need that you have. While we have the right to need what we need, *we do not have the right to expect to have that need met by another person.* The other person has the right to say "no." There can be a variety of reasons why the person is unable or unwilling to meet our need. This is an opportunity for further discussion, growth and deeper understanding. It also can be a deal breaker. Either way, when discussing and negotiating needs and boundaries we need to be open to differing feelings and needs from the other parties.

✓ Seek professional help to support healthy behavioral changes in regard to your anger.

✓ If you blow up at someone or misuse anger, take responsibility and apologize. Make a commitment to working on your relationship with anger and to use its power responsibly.

✓ Make external changes to your life to support better physical (exercise/nutrition) and mental health whatever that looks like to you.

**Forgiveness**

*"To forgive is to set a prisoner free and discover that the prisoner was you." – Lewis B. Smedes*

What if the boundary violator that you need to communicate with is dead? Or what if the person is still alive but you know that they are not open to having a constructive conversation? Then the answer is forgiveness.

Although most often connected with anger, forgiveness can be used with any of the primary feelings. The process of forgiveness cuts through the strings of unresolvable feelings, allowing us to free ourselves so that we can move forward.

Buddha said, "Holding onto anger is like drinking poison and expecting the other person to die." No matter how righteous the anger, if you cannot bring about a positive resolution then forgiveness is the best possible action, especially for you.

There are a lot of misconceptions about forgiveness, so let's be clear about what forgiveness is and what it isn't:

✓ Forgiveness is not about excusing or agreeing with what someone did.

✓ It is definitely not about forgetting what was done.

We want to learn and remember so that we don't
repeat the same mistakes.

✓ You do not have to like a person to forgive them.
Forgiving them does not mean you have to have a
relationship with them or have them in your life.

✓ Forgiveness is not about them at all!

✓ Forgiveness is all about us!

✓ Forgiveness is freedom for you.

Forgiveness is saying, "I honor the anger that I feel. I
have a right to be angry about what you did to me. It was
not fair, and it was not right. I also realize that there will be
no justice to be had in this situation and that carrying
around this anger is only hurting me. I cannot control what
you did. I can control how you affect me now, and I am
choosing to release this anger, so I am no longer burdened
by what you did. I am giving myself permission to get on
with my life. I am setting myself free!"

Give yourself permission to learn from what happened
and set yourself free to move on.

## Final Thoughts

*"There's nothing wrong with anger provided you use it
constructively." – Wayne Dyer*

Anger is an incredibly powerful tool that brings a lot of
clarity and empowerment to situations. Within every angry
experience, there is an opportunity to create or destroy, to
empower or disempower. Protection of what is important to
us is not achieved by being a doormat or from being a

bully. A state of peace is achieved with clearly communicated boundaries, honest discussions about what we
need, and negotiations to figure out how to create win/win
situations, whether they be intimate or professional in
nature. Anger is always looking out for us, making sure that
what is important to us is secure and letting us know when
we need to make an adjustment. The next time that anger
sets off your internal alarm, welcome it. Address the issue
that triggered it, unpack the feeling and use what you learn
to help you create healthier boundaries so that you can
experience more peace and respect in your life.

# CHAPTER 5
# FEAR

## Creating Safety

*"I'm not afraid of storms, for I'm learning how to sail my ship." – Louisa May Alcott*

Nancy wakes up every morning after a fitful night's sleep with a pit in her stomach. She worries about everything, a sick feeling of dread following her throughout her day. Even when there is nothing wrong, she can't shake the anxiety that stalks her. In her happiest moments, there is always a shadow of fear waiting for the other shoe to drop.

Jim is walking across a parking lot when there is a loud bang to his right. Jim crouches, his heart racing, panting, his eyes darting around, as he looks for the shooter. For a moment, he is somewhere else, lost in a memory of war. While his brain finally realizes that it was just a car backfiring, he can't control his body or his fear, as he spirals into a panic.

Around the age of 11, I started learning to horseback ride and jump English style. Although I was a good Western style horse rider, jumping was a very new and frightening activity. My fear would translate into what my British trainer Tony would call my "electric bum." The horses could feel my anxiety and would become nervous themselves, resulting in them running away with me. If you have ever tried to stop a runaway horse, then you know that it is like a pea trying to stop a rolling watermelon. It wasn't pretty and ended with me clinging for dear life until the horse had run itself out and finally slowed. It was terrifying, and I wasn't learning very much spending all my time trying to survive the lessons. Tony, my ever practical and wise trainer, watched this happen several days in a row and finally took me aside. What he shared with me that day has shaped my life ever since when it comes to fear. "When you're out of control" he advised, "stop trying to fight what you don't have control over. If you want control in an uncontrollable situation, accept what you can't control and control what you can. You can control you." The next day, Tony put me on an especially sensitive horse named Wispa. She had taken off with me every time I'd ridden her, and that day wasn't any different. At first, I started to panic, then I thought of what Tony had told me. I figured it was worth trying, so I took a deep breath, stopped fighting, and focused on controlling myself. Not fighting the situation allowed me to stop feeding my panic. This created space for me to think more clearly so that I could realize that I wasn't dying, which allowed me to calm down. I could feel Wispa calming as well once I wasn't pulling and flapping and clinging to her in terror. The more I controlled myself, the more control the horse gave back until we were flying across the ground completely under my direction. I learned a huge life lesson that day – fighting to control the uncontrollable is setting ourselves up for terror and failure. Creating safety is not about trying to control the uncontrollable storm or horse or life itself; it's about learning to control and trust in ourselves.

Being safe is a huge survival issue, and fear is the healthy response that keeps us out of danger. Without safety, there is no stability for us to grow or learn or build our life upon. Because of this, fear holds a lot of weight in our emotional world. It tells us to stay back from the cliff edge, run from danger, and be cautious of the unknown, which might hurt us. It is the flight of the fight-or-flight response. Safety and trust in ourselves and our surroundings is paramount to our ability to create a thriving life.

## Fear Gone Wrong

Fear has a practical job. It is meant to warn and get us away from danger as well as keep us cautious when encountering new and unknown factors. Fear becomes unhealthy when it becomes a way of life instead of being connected to an actual threat.

When we have fearful experiences in childhood or very traumatic events later in life – whether physical, mental, sexual or emotional – they tend to make a big impact. If we experienced not being safe as a child, if our needs (physical, mental or emotional) were not met on a regular basis, if we experienced abuse of any kind, or if we were physically or emotionally abandoned, then we learned on a deep level that we are not safe. Likewise, if we experience a traumatic event such as war, rape, robbery or an accident, that too can create a pattern of fearful behavior.

Whether our fear comes from an unsafe environment or

a traumatic life event, we can internalize the fearful experiences becoming hypervigilant, always on the lookout for potential threats. At this point, we don't need a "reason" to be afraid, as we live in a constant state of what I call "free floating" anxiety. Fear becomes our knee-jerk response to any situation because we don't know how to make ourselves safe. We think that if we can control what is happening around us then we might be able to finally feel secure. Trying to control life and all its variables will yield about as much success as I had stopping a 1000-pound horse, which is to say no success at all. We can't control life or other people, only ourselves and our actions.

As we unpack the experience of fear, we should always keep what we can control and what we can't control at the front of our minds.

**Unpacking Fear**

**Identify the Feeling**: First we must identify the feeling. If you would describe what you are feeling with any of these words than you may be working with fear – *worried, fearful, doubtful, anxious, unsure, scared, timid, terrified, shy, shaky, cowardly, menacing, wary, threatened, nervous, panic, alarmed, suspicious, stressed or paranoid.*

**Identify the Need**: We have identified that we are feeling fear which means there is an unmet need around safety and trust.

**Identify Cause**: What type of safety issue are we dealing with? There are three main category of threats that we must distinguish amongst. The first two are part of our survival process. It is in the third category, internal fears, where the most work lies. As always it is important for us to identify what type of fear or what combination of fears we are experiencing, only then will we know how to respond.

**External Threat:** These threats come from an *external source* that is *acting upon us*. A person attacking us physically or verbally, a bear chasing us, a natural disaster, war, or other dangerous events. These are the situations for which fear was created. Similar to anger, fear will alert you to the danger and give you the energy and strength to take action.

**Immediate Action:** When we are threatened like this, we must make split second decisions to save ourselves. There is not usually a lot of time to unpack the experience, we must run, hide, or fight to be safe. Once we are safe from the danger, then we can make time to unpack the experience to decide whether there are changes we can make to be safer in the future. For example, you experience an earthquake. Afterwards, you decide to buy a emergency kit for your home, office and car in case it happens again. You can't stop earthquakes, but you can take positive steps toward having what you need should another one occur.

**Unknowns Threat:** This is when we feel afraid because something is new and we don't have the skill set or experience to feel safe yet. In this case, fear is not saying "don't do it" but rather "be careful and learn more." Once we have more information, we can decide if the "unknown" is a danger or not.

**Action:** Remember how nervous you were the first

time you tried something new, like flying or driving a car or horseback riding? The way we transform our fears around new experiences is through learning and repetition. The trick is to expose ourselves to new experiences in a supportive way so that we have a positive experience. Every new successful experience expands our world and creates ever greater feelings of safety and trust in ourselves and in the process.

**Internal Threat:** Internal fear *originates within* us. These are the fears that are either born from our own minds or from past external experiences that are over now but that we have internalized. Internal fears don't need external stimulus although external situations can trigger or exaggerate them. When we have internalized fear(s) it has become a habit, a way of reacting to the world. Internalized fears become anxiety disorders such as chronic anxiety, panic attacks, obsessive compulsive disorder, post traumatic disorder, paranoia, and phobias.

**Self-reflection: questions to ask yourself**

- Do you know what has caused you to feel unsafe? Is it something you can control?
- What were you thinking about just before you felt the fear?
- What were you doing, watching or reading right before you felt the fear?
- Are you allowing fear causing influences in your life? Things like watching news, sugar, caffeine, alcohol, not enough sleep, and not enough exercise can all cause feelings of anxiety.
- Are there any specific changes you can make to

create a safer experience or environment for yourself in general?
- Are you feeling any fear that isn't yours?
- Are you anticipating an unsafe situation? For people with social anxiety, for example, an upcoming event can trigger anxiety days before the event takes place.
- Are you using all the resources that are at your disposal?

## Time to Take Action
### Internal Actions:

✓Make sure you support your physical well-being through exercise, nutrition and enough sleep.

✓Soothing self-talk: We all have self-talk. Be aware of how you speak to yourself and use kind and encouraging self-talk. When we are anxious, we make it worse by telling ourselves fearful stories and worrying over situations that are out of our control. Better to focus your thoughts on what you can control and remind yourself that you can only live in the moment. Here is some soothing self-talk around fear: "I am aware that I am feeling a lot of fear right now. Some of this fear is around stuff I have no control over. No amount of worrying is going to help me, I know that now. Am I safe right now? Yes, in this moment I am ok. I can only live in the present moment, and right now I am ok. I will take positive action on the items I can control. When I think about it, my life is actually pretty safe, and I am safe in this moment." Connecting yourself to the here and now stops you from projecting into the future or past where you are powerless to affect change. All we can control is ourselves in this moment.

✓ Replace fearful beliefs with beliefs about your overall safety and trust in life, yourself and/or a higher power.

✓ Release any fear that isn't yours.

✓ Start a meditation practice.

✓ Practice gratitude.

✓ Learn breathing techniques that help to calm and ground you. One technique I use often with clients is to put both feet on the ground and imagine that you can inhale and exhale through your feet. This helps pull your energy down into your body and ground you.

✓ Place a notebook by your bed where you can list action items that you need to remember so that you can rest at night instead of worrying about keeping everything in your head.

✓ Journaling is another way to help get what's in your head out. The act of writing down our fears can aid you in gaining some distance and being able to "see" what it is that you are thinking and worrying about.

✓ Play Worst-Case Scenario: A client I worked with had moderately severe social anxiety in which even small gatherings often lead to panic. When a family event came along, it was the perfect opportunity for her to practice creating safety for herself. We played the Worst-Case Scenario, and this is what it looked like:

### Family Event Case Scenario

| Worse Case: What you are afraid will happen | Prevention: What actions can you take beforehand? | After the fact: if the worst happens then what? | What I will miss out on if I don't go to the party |
|---|---|---|---|
| I will get overwhelmed and have a panic attack in front of everyone. | I can find a place to sit and let people come to me instead of feeling like I have to connect with everyone.<br><br>I will use soothing self-talk leading up to the party reminding myself of all the positive reasons why I want to go.<br><br>I will practice my breathing and meditating daily to help me stay grounded leading up to the event.<br><br>I will make sure to have some of my medication just in case. | If I start to feel overwhelmed, I will use my breathing practice to help me stay connected.<br><br>If I start to panic, I will go to a bathroom or bedroom away from people until I feel calmer.<br><br>I will take my medications if nothing else has helped.<br><br>I will ask my cousin for help. She knows about my social anxiety and is very sympathetic. | I will miss out on a fun time.<br><br>I won't get to celebrate with my family.<br><br>I won't get the chance to experience my family's love and support.<br><br>I will miss out on an opportunity to practice my ability to create safety for myself. |

## External Actions:

✓Limit or eliminate negative influencing including media, radio, books and movies. Be responsible for what you allow into your experience. Choose positive and uplifting influences.

✓ Limit time with people who are very anxious, negative, angry or sad. Choose to surround yourself with positive, confident and kind friends and family.

✓ Join a support group.

✓ Remove yourself from the stimulus until you are feeling calmer.

✓ Focus on what you can do and practice letting the rest go. Practice saying these types of things out loud to yourself and to friends. We verbalize what we believe so speaking new beliefs will help them to gain power in our minds.

✓ Get professional help to face past experiences that may be at the core of your internalized fear.

✓ Empower yourself by actively searching out and learning new skills and tools to use for when you are feeling anxious or in a state of stress or panic.

✓ Try new experiences, build your confidence and begin expanding your comfort zone. Start small and celebrate success.

**Final Thoughts**

*"Grant me the serenity to accept the things I cannot change, courage to change the things I can, and the wisdom to know the difference." – Serenity Prayer*

Fear is a good thing when it helps us avoid external dangers, but internalized fear is an unhealthy pattern that can lead to any number of disorders that stop us from living our lives to the fullest. When we realize that the answer to creating safety is about controlling us, our thoughts, beliefs and actions and not controlling the world, the power is placed back in our hands. When we turn our focus inward and practice self-control, we learn to trust in our own abilities to weather whatever may be thrown at us. When we learn to control ourselves, we also open ourselves to the awe, joy and empowerment that many of those uncontrollable life situations offer. I never would have experienced the thrill and freedom of riding a horse at top speeds across the English countryside had I not learned to let go of trying to control the uncontrollable and learned to trust in myself.

# CHAPTER 6
# LONELINESS

## Building Connection

*"At the innermost core of all loneliness is a deep and powerful yearning for union with one's lost self."*
*– Brendan Behan*

Dave is the life of any party. Popular, good looking, charming, successful. Everyone wants to be Dave or at least be around him. What his friends and colleagues can't imagine is that behind that confident smile Dave fears being alone with himself. He can't stand the feeling of emptiness inside, the loneliness that gnaws at him. Dave can't decide which is worse; being physically alone or feeling lonely in a crowd.

Being on her own is what Lucy does well. It's relationships with other people that she avoids. Growing up a military brat, moving every few years, she learned that connecting to other people leads to painful goodbyes and a broken heart. Older now, Lucy wants to learn how to be comfortable connecting with other people again, find someone to share her life with and start a family.

***

When May first came to see me, she told me a common story of loneliness and desperate attempts for connection.

"I have spent years trying to find a relationship that can

answer the emptiness that I feel inside…years of begging people to be with me. And it seems like I just kept getting the same kind of person, just like my parents, completely emotionally unavailable. The more alone I feel in a relationship, the more desperate I become to gain their affection. I'm always the needy one. I'm a sixty-seven-year-old woman; you'd think I would have figured it out by now."

Loneliness is the messenger of our deep need for connection. There are two types of disconnection – a disconnection within ourselves from ourselves and a disconnection from the outside world and other people. We often focus on our connection or lack thereof with other people, and while that is important, it is our connection to ourselves that is the foundation upon which all other connections are based. If we are feeling lonely, the first place we need to build connection is in our own selves.

**Disconnection – How it happens**

We learn at an early age to distance and disconnect ourselves from certain feelings, particularly those deemed unacceptable or bad by our parents, peers, society or religion. In the process of learning to deny and ignore what we feel/need, we end up afraid of ever actually being with ourselves in case we may have to acknowledge that those unacceptable feelings and needs are still there. Denying and ignoring our feelings and needs is a form of self-rejection. How can we hope to connect with another person's experience if we cannot connect with our own feelings and needs first? Like my client May, we can spend a lot of time desperately searching for that person or thing outside ourselves to fill the emptiness that only we can heal.

"I thought you were a bit crazy when you told me I needed to have a relationship with myself," May told me several months into our work together. "I mean, I'm with myself all the time, how can I not have a relationship with myself? But then I started to understand how I had learned to completely deny my feelings and needs and how I didn't know how to be with myself at all."

Taking the time to get to know ourselves opens the door for deep healing. Realizing that we don't need anyone else to feel a sense of belonging and connection frees us to make external connections based on sharing joy instead of trying to fill unmet needs.

### Unpacking Loneliness

**Identify the Feeling**: First, we must identify the feeling. If you were to describe what you are feeling with any of these words than you may be working with loneliness – *alone, isolated, disconnected, rejected, unwanted, desperate, needy, desolate, deserted, abandoned, adrift, apart, outcast, forsaken, empty.*

**Identify the Need**: We have identified that we feel lonely, which means there is an unmet need around connection.

**Identify Cause:** What type of disconnection are we dealing with? Disconnection from self? Disconnection from others? Both?

**Self-reflection: Questions to ask yourself if the disconnect is with yourself**

• Do you spend any time on your own?

• Are you afraid to spend time on your own? What are you afraid will happen or that you will feel if you spend time with yourself?

• Are you giving yourself permission to care about how you feel?

• Are you treating your needs like they matter?

• Do you have a sense of belonging in and to yourself?

**Self-reflection: Questions to ask yourself if the disconnect is with others**

• Are you involved in activities that nourish you?

• Are you involved in a community?

• Do you have causes or work that inspires you?

• Do you have a sense of belonging in the world?

• Are you wanting to connect to others out of lack/ need or because you have an abundance of joy/passion to share?

**Time to Take Action**
**Internal Actions:**

✓ Spend time every day with yourself. If the very idea gives you the heebie-jeebies, then you know this is an issue for you. Even 100% extroverts need time on their own to reflect and listen to their inner voice. Connection is created through real caring, so ask yourself throughout the day "What am I feeling?" and listen to the answer carefully.

✓ Address your feelings/needs as they arise. Treat yourself like you matter!

✓Use soothing and positive self-talk. No one wants to spend time with someone who judges and berates them. Use encouraging, positive and inspirational self-talk.

✓Replace old beliefs that make you feel alone or like you deserve to be alone with new beliefs that support your connection and belonging.

✓When you realize that you have fallen back into an old pattern of ignoring your feelings and needs, don't beat up on yourself. Instead, start reconnecting again by checking in with the feelings that you have been ignoring. Changing old patterns around distracting from our feelings takes time. The important thing is to keep recommitting to ourselves.

✓Fifteen minutes of daily meditation is helpful in rebuilding connection with yourself.

✓Stop using your "alone" status as an excuse to hide from life. Go to the museum you've wanted to see, go to the movies on your own, take that adult class that seemed interesting.

✓Work through any other feelings that are keeping you from connecting to yourself or others. Fear, for example, of future heartbreak or pain.

**External Action:**

✓Join clubs and communities that stand for causes or activities that are close to your heart and nourish you.

✓Give your time to a charity. We often get stuck focusing on what we lack instead of what we can give. There are many lonely people out there that feel isolated and unreachable. Join a charity that helps to reach out to vulnerable communities like seniors, the seriously ill, veterans, or animal shelters. Be the connection for someone else that you'd like in your own life.

✓Join a networking group.

✓Put yourself out there and try new activities, classes, and social events.

## Final Thoughts

*"Loneliness is the poverty of self; solitude is the richness of self." – May Sarton*

Connection and a sense of belonging is an important key to our happiness. We need both connection with self and with others to experience true fulfillment. When we reunite with our own feelings and needs first, we cultivate a foundation that supports us, as we extend ourselves out into the world. When we feel at home in ourselves we are available for a deeper experience of connection with others. Creating bonds within and without take commitment. We connect with what is important to us so the very best way to start building more connection is to invest more in both ourselves and the activities and causes that matter most to us.

# CHAPTER 7 - PAIN

## Call for Awareness

*"We fear violence less than our own feelings. Personal, private, solitary pain is more terrifying than what anyone else can inflict." – Jim Morrison*

Joan swallows another pill, washing it down with a shot of OJ. It's just the start of another day that she has to survive, another day pretending she has it all together. All she really cares about is finding relief. Right now, the pills are helping, but soon she will have to find something stronger. Something stronger to help her forget the abuse and all the pain, anger, shame and sadness it brings up.

Sam hit the snooze button for the fourth time. He knows he will be late to work but can't seem to care. He can't remember the last time he truly cared about anything. It all seems so pointless, especially since his marriage ended. Everything that used to be so important just seems...so irrelevant now. Tired to his core, all Sam wants is to sleep and not deal with anything.

\*\*\*

My teenage years were a struggle. My life at the time filled me with anger and overwhelming feelings of help-lessness and hopelessness. At some point, it was too much, and I remember a moment when all the pain imploded into a deep numbness. For months, I went through the motions watching myself from some distant place inside. Then one day I found myself sitting on the ledge of my window, my legs dangling, overlooking New York City from 31 stories high. I remember a voice inside my head saying, "Are we doing this?" in a very bored and unattached way. Did I want to die? No, but I couldn't keep living the way I had been. I sat on the ledge for a long time, and when I decided to climb back in, I also decided that I had to make changes to my situation or else I would find myself on that ledge again. To this day, I can't tell you what made me choose to turn away instead of jumping. I can tell you, though, that had I not made a change the likelihood of me making a different decision the next time I found myself on a ledge was very high.

Like a chirping fire alarm letting us know we need to change the batteries or flashing emergency lights, pain alerts us to where we need to bring our awareness – physically, mentally, emotionally or spiritually. If pain could speak, it would say, "Hey! Stop! There is something here that needs your awareness and attention!"

In general, we are a pain-phobic society, quick to avoid pain, emotional or otherwise. If the problem isn't easily fixed, we have little patience for investigating what our pain may be trying to bring to our attention. We'd rather find a distraction or use a quick Band-Aid of a solution rather than delve into our pain.

### Pain Gone Wrong

Pain goes wrong when we don't listen, then it starts to build. Pain often partners with the other primary feelings to add an urgency to unmet need(s). The more rejected, unresolved feelings we have, the more pain builds until it becomes a continual presence in our life. Long held, deeply charged, neglected feelings can begin to bleed into one horrific, silent scream of unending pain. To live in that kind of emotional pain is unbearable for any length of time. There are three common ways that we cope when pain reaches these levels:

• **Depression**: Depression is a state of suffering in which we shut down by disconnecting and disassociating from our ourselves, so that we can find relief in a state of numbness. When we are depressed, we are a shadow of ourselves – flat, numb, deeply depleted and devoid of that spark that makes us *us*. This deep disconnection can destroy everything we are involved in – jobs, marriages, families – leading to even more pain and even more reasons for us to retreat. Depression is a danger sign telling us that whatever we have been doing is not working! We must find a new way of working with our feelings and needs immediately.

• **Addiction:** Addiction looks for relief in the form of distractions. There are plenty of distractions to choose from – food, pills, social media, alcohol, drugs, work, sex, shopping, TV. Just about anything can be used as a distraction, and in and of themselves distraction can be neutral so long as they are used moderately. Distractions become a problem when we use them to escape what we are feeling with no clear plan of returning to deal with whatever made us want to escape in the first place. When we use an activity or substance as an escape instead of a conscious tool, it will lead us into a destructive cycle – feel badly, distract, feel better for as long as the distraction lasts, then feel badly again. We will need ever greater distractions to escape our ever-growing feelings. Let's be honest, we all have our preferred method of escaping painful feelings, something we turn to to provide us temporary relief. Like depression, addiction is a symptom of unresolved pain and feelings, and we as addicts need to learn to use healthier resources to help actually address the issues instead of just trying to escape them.

• **Suicide**: Most people who choose suicide don't want to die, they just want the pain to stop. By the time suicide is seriously considered, most have tried to find other ways to alleviate the pain all to no avail. It seems hopeless and helpless. For a person to consciously override their unconscious' primary directive to survive at all cost means their suffering is unbearable. This is an important reminder of how vital the quality of our relationship is to our feelings and needs. Seek help if you are even contemplating suicide. As someone who has been on that ledge, I can tell you that life holds so much more than pain. You and life are worth another chance.

**Unpacking Pain**
**Identify the Feeling**: If you can describe what you are feeling with any of these words, then you may be working with pain – *tormented, heartbroken, pained, crushed, tortured, desolate, dejected, rejected, afflicted, wronged, worthless, numb, lifeless, offended, harassed, unheard,*

*stressed, unwanted, invisible, overlooked, overwhelmed, helpless, hopeless.*

**Identify the Need**: We have identified that we are feeling pain, which means there is a need for awareness.

**Identify Cause:** What needs our attention?

**Self-reflection: questions to ask yourself**

- What do you need to become aware of?
- Why is this causing you pain?
- What have you been avoiding lately?
- What other feelings is the pain bringing to your attention?
- Is there a lesson to learn?
- Are you self-medicating with drugs, food, alcohol, shopping, sex, work or any other distraction?
- What action or change could you make?
- Is the pain overwhelming; do you need help?
- Are you using all the resources available to you?

**Time to Take Action:**

**Internal Action(s):**

- ✓ Pay attention! Listen to yourself. Give yourself permission to care about what hurts you emotionally, mentally and physically. Learn to listen early so that you can answer the whispers of pain instead of waiting until it is screaming.
- ✓ Take care of any other feelings that are connected to the pain and address your needs.
- ✓ Support yourself physically, mentally and emotionally. Make your health a priority.
- ✓ Daily exercise has been shown to help reduce

depression.

✓Nutrition also has been shown to affect mood. Food is medicine. Seek help to find out what foods are best for your particular issues.

✓Get out into nature. Remind yourself that there is a big, beautiful world out there.

✓Take note of any lessons you can learn from the situation so that you can bring greater awareness in future situations.

✓Daily mindfulness and meditation practices have been shown to help manage both emotional and physical pain and to reduce depression.

✓Practice gratitude. Start the day with the words "Thank you" and find one thing, no matter how small, to appreciate.

✓Use soothing positive self-talk. Stop blaming and beating up on yourself. Practice being kind to yourself.

✓Replace painful beliefs. Life can be good and easy and full of joy.

**External Action(s):**

✓Seek professional support! Don't wait, be proactive. This is very important for those experiencing depression, addiction or contemplating suicide.

✓Ask for help from trusted friends and family. People often are afraid of being burdens on their loved ones. Talk to those same loved ones, and they will tell you that they would rather you asked for help then that you suffered on your own.

✓Learn to communicate with your family and friends.

Remember that most people don't know how to deal with their own feelings let alone yours. Let people know what you need from them. Often, they are willing to give you what you need but won't know what to give on their own and will need you to spell it out.

✓If you and your doctor decide that medication is appropriate to manage your emotional pain (anti-depression or anti-anxiety medications), don't stop your inner work. The medication is there to help while you continue to search for the source of the pain so that you can heal it.

✓Be extremely picky about who you allow into your environment. Let go of people, family, jobs or anything else that is negatively influencing you and/or causing you pain.

✓Seek out positive influences.

✓Engage in nourishing and supportive activities both alone and in groups.

### Final Thoughts

*"There is no birth of consciousness without pain."*
*– Carl Jung*

Pain, like all feelings, is just a messenger not the mes-sage itself. Life need not be about pain and suffering. Like a flashing neon sign, pain is letting us know we are headed into suffering states, the opposite direction from where we want to go. When we understand pain's purpose as a messenger of long unanswered needs, we don't have to fear it so much. Pain then can become a prelude to deeper under-standing, self-awareness and positive course corrections that will lead us out of suffering and back into well-being.

# CHAPTER 8
# SADNESS

## Letting Go

*"You cannot protect yourself from sadness without
protecting yourself from happiness."*
*– Jonathan Safran Foer*

Ron cared for his wife during her terminal illness. Eigh-teen months of drawn out grief and goodbyes leave Ron feeling like he has already used up his time for grieving. If that's true, then why is he still so sad now, months after her death? Her death wasn't a surprise, and unlike many people, he and his wife got to say everything they needed to before her death. Ron figures he has no reason to be sad and finds that not talking or thinking about it works best in helping him shake it off.

Within a 3-year span, Monica falls in love, marries, and gives birth to a beautiful child. When she has everything she's ever wanted, why does she think about the independent, free life she used to live and cry? Confused herself and afraid that her husband won't understand, Monica tries to hide her sadness from him and herself.

\*\*\*

For several years, I volunteered at an amazing nonprofit in Tucson called Tu Nidito. It was there while helping seriously ill and grieving children that I had to work through my own prejudices and fears around sadness and began to honor the process of grief.

At Tu Nidito, we used a combination of talking circles and play therapy with the children. We would sit in a big circle, pose a question like "What do you miss most about the person?" or "Is there anything you wish you had been able to tell them?" and passed around a talking stick. The child with the talking stick could speak or pass. When they spoke, we listened. We didn't try to comfort them or make it better. We didn't tell them it was going to be ok or not to be sad. We didn't even make comforting sounds. We just listened with our hearts and ears open. And when they were done speaking, we said, "Thank you for sharing."

At first, it seemed strange, almost cold, not to comfort them. It wasn't long before I realized, though, that the normal "comforting" we offer, even with the best of intentions, is really a "shushing" mechanism. By *not* trying to "make it better," it allowed the person the space to feel whatever they are feeling for as long as they needed to feel it.

Sadness is the messenger of loss and change. If we feel sad, then it means that we have lost something important to us and need to process the loss, to face the change, and to let go of what was so that we can be present to what is.

We like to believe that we can control the outside world and that if we hold on tight enough we can keep things the way they are. Losses fly in the face of those illusions and bring home the fact that nothing is forever. We live in an ever-changing world and that terrifies us. No matter how much we try to control it or how hard we hold fast, people die, hearts break, illness happens, betrayal exists, jobs change, friendships fade, and life goes on.

Sometimes we see loss coming a mile away, dreading it as it gets closer and closer, like someone suffering a terminal illness or when we may be leaving our family to go away for work or deployment.

Sometimes loss blindsides us – a sudden death, a diagnosis, loss of a job, or betrayal from someone close.

Sometimes it slips in the backdoor and sidles up to us when we least expect it, like when sadness and excitement come together around times of life transitions such as moves, job changes, having a baby or getting married. We may be happy about what is coming next but also feel sadness about the loss of the life that we knew up to that point.

Sometimes we tap into the greater universal feelings of loss and feel our hearts aching for the state of our world, our country, the animals, or the environment.

When we stop to take notice, we find that sadness seems to stalk us through life. That makes sense when you think about it; life is change, and where there is change there is a constant flow of beginnings and endings, losses and gains, life and death. Life is really a series of letting go.

## Grief

*"The most painful state of being is remembering the future, particularly the one you'll never have."*
*– Soren Kierkegaard*

Sadness is the feeling – the need is to let go – the way to fulfill that need is through grief.

Grief is a process that can include different states of suffering and many feelings – anger, pain, loneliness, fear and, of course, sadness. Sadness is the one constant feeling of grief, our guide through the grieving process.

### Sadness Gone Wrong

If we try to circumvent the grieving process, as we often do, we end up getting stuck. Here are two common ways in which we can become entangled in sadness.

**Grief Deniers:** Deniers either feel that grief has a specific time limit or that they aren't entitled to feel grief at all. They often belittle their feelings of loss, put a "happy face" on it, and feel that they should "just get over it." Their overall attitude is to "shush" grief in themselves and in others. The problem in building a wall of denial around ourselves is that we end up cutting ourselves off from our own feelings and the love and support of friends and family who could help us heal. By denying ourselves time to work through the grieving process, we only postpone the inevitable and draw out the grieving process instead of shortening it.

**Grief Stricken:** The opposite response to grief is equally damaging: those who define themselves by their grief and won't let go. These people hang onto the loss as a connection to the past, and it becomes an excuse to not move forward. Withdrawing from friends, work and activities they used to enjoy the grief-stricken person can fall into a deep hole of grief that may last for decades without relief. A client who lost her son in a car accident told me, "I feel like if I let this go that I will lose him forever. I need to grieve him to honor him." Another client with cancer who become stuck in the anger phase of her grieving process said, "If I let go of the anger it's like I am saying that it's ok that I got sick."

Holding onto grief doesn't help or honor anyone and can seriously hurt the grieving person. Like forgiveness, grief is not about forgetting. It is not about saying that something that we lost was not important to us. Grief is a process that leads us into a new way of being that incorporates the changes that have happened and sets us free to be present to our lives now. When we fight the process of grief and get stuck, all we see is the loss, the door that has closed, and we miss out on all the doors that are opening. Grief teaches us about honoring where we have been so that we can welcome what comes next, to let go of what is already gone so we can be present to what is.

## Unpacking Sadness

**Identify the Feeling**: If you would describe what you feel with any of these words, then you may be working with sadness – *sorrowful, pained, grieved, desolate, alone, sad, tearful, heartbroken, mournful, dismayed, anguish.*

**Identify the Need**: We have identified that we are feeling sadness which means there is a need to process an important loss through grief and let go.

**Identify Cause:** What or who have we lost?

**Self-reflection: questions to ask yourself**

- What or who did you lose?
- What did they or it mean to you?
- Have you given yourself permission to grieve?

- What are you afraid will happen if you allow yourself to grieve?
- Are you clinging to your grief? How do you think holding onto your grief will benefit you?
- Are you feeling anyone else's sadness?
- In what ways did the thing or person change you by being in your life?
- Are you using all the resources, connection and tools at your disposal?

**Time to Take Action**
**Internal Action(s):**

✓Let yourself feel what you feel without denying it or ignoring it or holding on to it. Just let those feelings, whatever they may be, flow through you. It means being kind to yourself and admitting that you hurt.

✓Remind yourself that there is nothing too small to grieve. Feeling sad is natural when we lose something that is important to us.

✓Don't compare your grief to anyone else's. Everyone grieves in their own way and in their own time.

✓Soothe don't shush yourself with your self-talk. Tell yourself that it is ok to feel whatever you are feeling.

✓Don't put a time limit on your process. It might take minutes or years. It may seem complete and then, as my best friend puts it, "grief leaps out and mugs you when you least expect it." And there is some grief that will stay with us our entire life, becoming softer and worn with time but still there like a scar upon our hearts. Each experience is unique and needs to be honored as such.

✓In the face of uncontrollable loss, whatever that loss may be, we often look to regain a feeling of control by blaming ourselves. Be patient with yourself if this is the case. The need to be at fault will release as you work through the process. It is another layer of accepting the uncontrollable nature of loss.

✓Give yourself permission to feel more than one feeling at a time. We can feel sadness and joy at the same time without them taking away from or lessening the other.

✓If there are unsaid words between you and someone you have lost, whether they be positive or negative, write them a letter. It is important to release the words and not hold them inside.

✓Release any sadness that is not yours.

✓Support yourself physically – exercise, nutrition, sleep.

✓Practice gratitude even in loss.

✓Take time to meditate. It is important to invest in yourself during times of grief.

✓If sadness is more of a state of being than a feeling for you, then question your beliefs and replace them

with beliefs that encourage you to be present and to let go.

**External Action(s):**
✓Seek support from trained professionals or grief

groups.
- ✓ Ask your friends and family for their help when you need it.
- ✓ Gently remind friends and family that you don't need them to "make it better." You are ok with and processing your sadness. The best way they can support you is to simply listen and be with you.
- ✓ Celebrate the anniversaries of the loss if it feels right. Honor the fact that the person or thing that was in your life was important to you.
- ✓ Welcome others to speak about the person or thing lost and to share their memories and experiences with you.
- ✓ Honor loss by embracing life not hiding from it.

## Final Thoughts

*"There are things that we don't want to happen but have to accept, things we don't want to know but have to learn, and people we can't live without but have to let go."*
*– Unknown*

Accepting loss is never easy. Yet the journey from sadness to acceptance is full of valuable lessons that, if we allow them, will make life that much more beautiful in its complexity. As we acknowledge the loss and its affect upon us, we learn new ways of being without that person, relationship or thing while still honoring that we are forever changed for having experienced them in the first place. At its core, sadness is about learning to say "yes" to this ever-changing experience called life and reminds us that each moment is an opportunity to be embraced.

# CHAPTER 9
# SHAME

### Reclaiming Our Self-Worth

*"Shame is the intensely painful feelings that we are unworthy of love or belonging." – Dr. Brene Brown*

As a little boy, Jared was the wild one, the troublemaker, the cause of his family's problems. At least that's how the story always goes. All Jared knows for sure is that there has always been something wrong with him. He will never be as good as his other siblings or live up to the exacting standards of his parents. He often thinks that he'd be doing everyone a favor if he just took himself out of the equation.

"Stupid, stupid, stupid," Annie mutters to herself as she drives away from the job interview, sure that she completely screwed it up. She catches her own reflection in the rearview mirror, "Why can't you ever get anything right?!" Tears clog her throat; she is disgusted by herself.

\*\*\*

Once upon a time, a baby was born. Like all babies, it was precious, valuable and perfectly imperfect. The baby's parents and family doted upon the child not because of what the baby did (babies do very little of anything), but because the adults recognized in the baby its inherent worth as a precious little Being.

The child grew, like all children do, and the adults, like all adults do, began to teach the child what was right and what was wrong, what was allowed and what wasn't. These teachings were specific, as all teaching are, to the society, traditions, religions and culture that the child had been born into. The child, like all children, was an open book and took these teachings into itself as truths. This is exactly how the child's parents, when they were children, had learned the same "truths" that they were now teaching.

The child learned which feelings were acceptable and which ones were unacceptable, which needs were appropriate, and which ones to never mention. The child, like all children, only wanted to be accepted and to be loved, so the child did not question these teachings. Instead, the child took all the "bad" feelings, needs and personality traits and shut them up in a deep dark place inside. In this way, the child only showed the most acceptable face to the world.

As the child grew into adulthood, as all children do, there were more and more pieces that teachers, friends, religion and society found unacceptable. Each of these pieces had to be cut off and shoved into that dark place with the others. The child grew up to be a very acceptable adult who knew all the right things to feel, need, do and say. Having done all the "good" and "acceptable" things, the grown child was supposed to be happy and fulfilled. Why then did the grown child feel so lonely, so sad, so full of pain? Why did the grown child feel not good enough? As if there was something wrong on a fundamental level of their being.

That feeling, the one that tells you that you will never be enough, that there is something wrong with you, that you are not lovable, not worthy enough – that's shame.

Shame is unlike the other six primary feelings for one important reason – we aren't born with it. Anger, fear, joy, loneliness, pain and sadness are all a part of our natural guidance system, and we are born feeling them. The first time we feel shame, it has always been introduced from the outside first. Once experienced, shame is impossible to eradicate. Shame is the most powerfully destructive feeling, an emotional cancer that eats away at our inherent self-worth till we believe that we are worthless.

Shame is a lie that tells us that at our core there is something wrong with us and we are not good enough. That lie becomes so convincing that we completely forget our own value even though we may be able to recognize it in others. Shame is repellent; no one wants to feel it or own it. We want to be as far away as possible from it, which means when certain feelings, needs or personality traits are shamed, we not only reject them but are repelled by those parts of us. It's a recipe for despair: Our inborn feelings and needs that are there to help us connect to our natural state of well-being vs. a powerful lie that is introduced from the outside telling us that what we are naturally feeling, and needing is wrong, bad, unnatural, evil and/or disgusting. In other words, we are taught to be repelled by ourselves. Shame literally attacks us at our core, at our Being-ness.

## Shame is Always Wrong
If we are told that we are not good enough, then we have

two ways to deal with that. We can try to live up to expectations and become what we perceive those around us want us to be, becoming the Perfectionist, or we can live down to expectations and define ourselves by what people are telling us we are, the Delinquent.

**Perfectionist:** The Perfectionist must excel in all things. These are overachievers who demand perfection from themselves and from the people around them. They will juggle fifty balls, tap dance, sing and feel like a failure if they can't also do a backflip at the same time. While they may look like they have it all together, on the inside they are deeply suffering and can never admit it. We have done untold damage as a society by holding this type of overachieving behavior up as something to aspire to. The Perfectionist is a lie, and Perfectionists themselves know it. They have checked every box, run every race, aced every exam, gone for every golden star, and they are empty, unhappy, anxious and filled with pain. Once on the treadmill of perfection, they cannot stop no matter how unfulfilling, exhausting or harmful because if they stop then everyone would see behind their perfect façade to the "failure" underneath.

**Delinquent**: Ever heard of living down to expectations? In the face of deep shaming, Delinquents, unlike Perfectionists, decide either in rebellion or in despair that they aren't good enough so what's the point in trying to be? These are the black sheep, the one that everyone shakes their head at, muttering how they had such potential. While the Perfectionist is encouraged in their dysfunctional and self-harming behavior, the Delinquent is shunned and pitied as a failure, held up as an example of who not to be.

Unless we have done some serious shame work most of us will recognize ourselves in one or a mixture of both of these "types." The Perfectionist and Delinquent behavior is born from believing the lie that there was ever something wrong with us. Shame is so painful *because* it's message of unworthiness is so untrue and is at odds with our own inner knowing of self-worth.

There are three main strategies we need to implement in our lives to start tearing away the lies of shame:

1. **Stop comparing!** Comparison is the tool of shame. It's a lose/lose scenario – either we make ourselves feel better than someone else or we find ourselves less than another person. When we compare, we are buying into the lie. Each one of us is unique, celebrate your difference without having to compare.

2. **Embrace your imperfection**. We are born perfectly imperfect. You were never meant to be perfect. Perfection is stagnant and unchanging. We are born to grow and expand and learn. To be perfect is impossible for any living being. When we try to be perfect we set ourselves up for failure and feed into a never-ending cycle of shame. Practice being good enough instead.

3. **Disconnect worth from external conditions**. Every child, including you, was born with the same amount of worth. That worth remains the same throughout life no matter what. Self-worth is not attached to action of any kind. There is no amount of "do-gooding" that will increase your innate worth, and no

amount of "screwing up" will lessen it. Your worth is tied into the fact that you are a human being, a living consciousness, an extension of Source, the Universe, God or whatever word you use. And yes, that means that all living things have worth, and we should treat them accordingly. Likewise, no one can take away our worth, add to our worth, or hold our worth hostage although they may want us to think that they can. Nothing and no one can destroy our worth, but shame can certainly obscure it.

**Unpacking Shame**

**Identify the Feeling**: If you describe what you are feeling with any of these words, then you may be working with shame: *ashamed, bad, wrong, repugnant, abomination, disrespected, embarrassed, disgusting, diminished, less than, evil, detestable, powerless, unworthy, worthless, moron, monster, stupid, loser, a disappointment, useless, trash, unlovable.*

**Identify the Need**: We have identified that we feel shame, which means there is a need to remember our natural inborn worthiness.

**Identify Cause:** Who or what triggered the feeling of shame?

**External:** Is someone else trying to shame you?

**Internal:** Is the shame coming from inside?

**Combo:** Often someone can shame us and that will trigger old shame as well.

**Self-reflection: Questions to ask yourself**

• What did the other person(s) say that felt shameful?

Is this truly a reason to feel less than?
- Were you comparing yourself to someone else?
- What would happen if you didn't try to live up to other people's "shoulds," opinions or expectations?
- In trying to feel better, did you push shame onto someone else?
- Are you "doing" in hopes of getting love, recognition, or proving that you are good enough? What would happen if you stopped "doing" or trying to please?
- What feelings, needs or traits were you told are not allowed or that you needed to hide growing up?
- What if you stopped listening to what other people think about you and decide for yourself?

**Time to Act**
**Internal Action(s):**

Turn to look at the shame. As repellent as shame is the first step is to admit that we all have some and that doesn't make us bad or wrong. All of us have feelings of shame and the best thing we can do is look upon those feeling with deep compassion. Shame cannot survive long in the light of kindness and acceptance.

✓Question your motives. If you find yourself trying to please others or "doing" in hopes of receiving acceptance and worth, unwind the motives from the actions. Remind yourself that worth is not connected to outside conditions.

✓Question how you define yourself. If you are letting

other people tell you who you are, then it's time to start changing the narrative.

✓ Get a picture of yourself when you were very young and use it to remind you that you are still that precious, perfectly imperfect and worthy being.

✓ Practice pleasing yourself vs. always trying to please others.

✓ Use gratitude to stay focused on all your blessings.

✓ Meditate to help reconnect to your inner knowing.

✓ Replace shame-filled beliefs with beliefs that remind you of your worthiness. "I am" statement are particularly powerful as they are seen as a command by the unconscious mind. Be aware of what "I am" beliefs you tell yourself. Shame filled beliefs like "I am stupid," "I am unlovable," "I am bad," "I am never enough" are extremely damaging. Begin replacing these statements with worth filled beliefs such as "I am enough," "I am perfectly imperfect," "I am lovable," "I am loved," "I am unique," "I am blessed," "I am worthy of life and love."

✓ Use encouraging self-talk that reminds you of your inner goodness and value and delightful imperfection.

**External Action(s):**

✓ If you realize that you have shamed someone take responsibility for your actions and apologize. The cycle of shaming cannot be broken until each of us takes responsibility for ourselves. It is fine to disagree and call someone out on their actions, beliefs or opinions while being careful not to shame the person with name calling and judgement. "I disagree strongly with your stance on education reform" vs. "Only morons would think that!" or "You're just an awful person if you believe that."

✓If someone else shares something that they are ashamed of, listen, be kind and respond with compassion. Keep the advice to a minimum. What they need is your acceptance and empathy more than anything.

✓Be an amazing example of owning your imperfection. Practice being "good enough." Show people that imperfection is beautiful not something to shun.

✓Stay away from influences that feel shameful or people who shame.

✓Seek out positive, empowering and respectful influences.

✓Get professional help to sort through the shame and bring those parts of yourself that you rejected back into the light of consciousness.

## Final Thoughts

*"Shame needs three things to grow exponentially in our lives: secrecy, silence and judgment." –Dr. Brene Brown*

Shame, unfortunately, is everywhere. It has become the norm in entertainment, politics, religion, and in the way that we speak to each other and think about ourselves. The time has come to start calling out shame, in ourselves and when we see it in the world. When we do point it out, do it kindly, and with great compassion. Don't judge another person harshly; most of us are so immersed in shame that we don't even know that we are participating in it. It's important to go back and look at what feelings, needs and traits we were lead to believe are bad in ourselves and in other people. We can explore those rejected parts, reintroduce ourselves, questions why we were told to cut those pieces out in the first place. Shame work is extremely uncomfortable but incredibly rewarding, as we recover parts of ourselves we thought lost forever and even discover new things about ourselves that we never imagined. Delve down deep enough, and you will find your innate worth still there, waiting for you to reclaim it.

# CHAPTER 10
# JOY

## Open Up and Receive!

*"Joy is what happens to us when we allow ourselves to recognize how good things really are."*
*– Marianne Williamson*

Relaxing in a beach chair in his backyard Zack's heart is filled with joy. The happy sounds of his kids playing in the sprinkler, the smell of hamburgers on the grill, the taste of a cold beer – life is good.

\*\*\*

When we feel joy, our feeling guidance system is telling us we are on the right path. Needs are being met. Alleluia!

Usually we think of a need as asking for something that is missing. Joy speaks to a different type of need – the type of need that asks for more. Joy's message encourages us to "open up, allow and receive more." The more joy we allow, the more joy we can receive. This is the one case in which the feeling is both the messenger and the message. When you feel joy you need more joy.

The purpose of all the primary feelings is to guide us into states of well-being. We don't want to experience just a little bit of these states, we want to *live* in these states as much of the time as we can. Joy is the messenger that keeps us moving from feeling good to feeling even better. If life were a game of hotter/colder the other primary feelings are telling us when we are getting colder, while joy is telling us we are hot on the trail of where we want to be.

**How can Joy possibly go wrong?**

Many of us are so unused to having our needs met and feeling good that when we start to feel joy it triggers any unmet needs that must be dealt with before we can fully accept and open ourselves to more joy. One client expressed this conundrum beautifully, "Everything was going so well. I was happy, my job, my relationship – I didn't trust it. It was like I was so unused to things going my way that I had to mess it up. I realized that I am more comfortable being uncomfortable. I don't know what do when all I have to do is feel good." Confronted with joy, many people feel that "things are going TOO well" or they are waiting for the "other shoe to drop." When we don't understand the purpose of feelings, then we can misinterpret this experience as our "bad" feelings sabotaging our happiness.

The needs that joy represent, to receive, to allow, and to share, by their very nature will activate any of the other unmet needs that still need honoring. How do we allow and receive when we are not in a place of trust, peace, belonging or self-worth? Whatever feeling is triggered by joy is highlighting where we need healing to move forward. This is another part of joys job – to show us what is keeping us from more joy. Instead of this being a "sabotage," it is an opportunity to unpack the feelings and take action to fulfill the needs they represent. If we do that, then we stay on course toward creating an ever increasing, joy-filled experience.

**Unpacking Joy**

**Identify the Feeling**: If you describe what you are feeling with any of these words, then you may be working with joy: *happy, light, encouraged, clear, bubbly, eager, appreciation, gratitude, daring, optimistic, free, joyful, cheerful, hopeful, supported, loved, connected, warm, secure, alive, ease, comfort, carefree.*

**Identify the Need**: We have identified that we are feeling joy which means we are on the right path and need to allow, receive and share the many blessing life has in store for us.

**Identify Cause**: Is there something in particular that sparked your joy or is it a general feeling of well-being?

**Self-reflection: questions to ask yourself**

✓Do you welcome joy or are you suspicious of it?

✓Do you enjoy seeing other people experience joy?

✓Would you describe yourself as a person who is a good receiver? Do you allow others to give to you?

✓Do you enjoy sharing? In general, do you believe and live in mindset of abundance believing that there is more than enough for everyone? Or do you believe and live in a scarcity mindset in which you are afraid that there won't be enough and that resources are limited?

✓What other primary feeling(s) are triggered when things are going well for you?

**Time to Take Action**

**Internal Action(s):**

✓Enjoy feeling joy! It may feel a bit strange, you

may not be used to it, but joy is a natural state and one that we have been seeking. Joy is for everyone. You can never have too much joy so open up, give yourself permission to feel good and when you are bursting, share it with those around you.

✓ Work through any triggered feelings/needs.

✓ Practice receiving in all areas of life.

✓ Practice an attitude of gratitude. You don't need to wait to feel joy to start focusing on the many things in your life that you appreciate from the smallest to the largest of blessings. Write down 3-5 things every day. Any time that you have a moment throughout the day look for reasons to be thankful.

✓ If you really want to take gratitude to the next level then practice what I call "Pre-ciation," which is when you are grateful for and appreciating the things that haven't happened yet but that you fully expect are on the way. It is easy to be thankful for what we already have. It takes a master of appreciation to be thankful in advance.

✓ Joyful self-talk – Talk up and point out to yourself all the joy, abundance, prosperity and blessings in your life.

✓ Breathe.

✓ Smile often.

✓ Find excuses to laugh.

✓ Get outside and glory in nature.

✓ Do nothing, laze in the grass, hug a tree, walk barefoot, watch sunsets, eat great food, pamper yourself, do something you've always wanted.

✓ Sing, dance, do something creative.
**External Action(s):**
✓ Share your joy.
✓ Give a compliment.
✓ Share a smile.
✓ Be a positive influence in other people's lives.
✓ Invite others to join you in joyful activities.

## Final Thoughts on Joy

*"Sometimes your joy is the source of your smile, but sometimes your smile can be the source of your joy."*
*– Thich Nhat Hanh*

Joy is easy if we will let it be. So, open up and say "yes!" to joy, to feelings, to honoring unmet needs, and living in states of well-being. Really, our feeling journey is all about meeting our needs to clear the way for more joy in our lives. Isn't now a great time to get started?!

# CHAPTER 11
# HEADED TOWARD WELL-BEING

*"You have brains in your head. You have feet in your
shoes. You can steer yourself any direction you choose.
You're on your own. And you know what you know. And
YOU are the one who'll decide where to go..."*
*– Dr. Seuss, Oh The Places You'll Go!*

I went on a hike with a mentor friend of mine several
years ago. We were quiet as we walked, enjoying the
feel of the early morning air, watching as the sun rose
over the mountains. At the top there was a vantage point
where we could look out over the Tucson valley. We sat
side by side lost in our own thoughts and the beauty laid
out before us. I was contemplating a crossroads in my life
and what I was going to do. I had a choice to make; one
way would lead me down a fairly safe route, and the other
would take me to some uncomfortable and unknown
places.

"When confronted with two paths, how do you decide
which one to take?" I asked suddenly.

My friend turned, threw his arm around me, and said,
"That's easy. Choose the one you feel least ready for."

We've come to the end of our journey, but it's the
beginning of a new one for you. There are two paths in
front of you and a choice to make. One path will lead you
down a familiar road, where you don't implement anything
you've learned in these pages and continue to ignore, deny

and avoid your feeling. Familiar and comfortable even in its discomfort, this path leads to the same places where you already live.

Then there is the other path, unknown, uncomfortable because it means doing things differently than you have before. It means turning toward your feelings and caring about how you feel and what you need. Although it is an unfamiliar path you now have the elements you need to travel this way. You now know:

- ✓ The fundamental answers to where feelings come from, what they are, and why they are important.
- ✓ The seven primary feelings and which needs each feeling is connected to.
- ✓ How to unpack your feelings to self-correct and realign with your natural states of well-being.
- ✓ Actions you can take both internally and externally to create real change.

Feeling a bit of fear at the beginning of a new venture is natural. You don't need to know, control or foresee exactly what awaits you on this new road because you have an inborn GPS – *your feelings*. You now know how to transform those feelings into a positive guidance system that addresses your needs and keeps you en-route to where you want to go. Time to implement what you've learned, trust and listen to your inner GPS and let it guide you down this new path toward the life of well-being that awaits you.

# RESOURCES

There are so many resources at our fingertips now. Here are a few examples of videos, books and apps that you can utilize for little to no money that may be helpful on your journey.

**Video**
YouTube, TEDX Talks

**Meditation Apps**
Calm, Guided meditations, Mindfulness, HeadSpace, Insight Timer, Smiling Mind

**Gratitude Apps**
Attitudes of Gratitude Journal, Secret of Happiness, Journey - Diary, Journal, Happier, The Gratitude Habit

**Exercise Apps**
Couch to 5k, Daily Workout, Perfect Workout, 5 Min. Home Workout

**Mental Health Apps**
Talkspace, Therapist Finder, My Psych

**Authors**
There are many inspirational authors with powerful messages, these are just a starting point: Abraham-Hicks,

Brene Brown, Louise Hay, Wayne Dyer, Marianne Williamson, Tony Robbins

## FREE BONUS
Free Worksheets Available for You:
WWW.ANXIOUSTOAWESOME.COM

# HIRE ALEXCIS TO SPEAK

If you host events or know someone who does, let's talk. One of my passions is speaking and I'd love to bring a healing message of inspiration to your corporation, association, group or church.

Email me (transformativetouch@gmail.com) and be sure to include the type, date, location and budget for your event in your message.

# ABOUT THE AUTHOR

Alexcis Spencer Lopez is a therapist and owner of A Transformative Touch Wellness Center. A mind-body healing specialist, Alexcis brings holistic healing to the root causes of emotional, mental and physical traumas. Alexcis writes and speaks on the topics of Feelings, Consciousness and Connection and is passionate about exploring alternate healing and spiritual traditions. She holds a BA in Philosophy, an MS in Metaphysics, and is a certified Hypnotherapist, certified Master Neuro-Linguistic Life Coach, Licensed Body-worker, Usui Reiki Master, ordained minister, and disciplined in Shamanism. A fun and engaging speaker, Alexcis has led many workshops over the years. Her writing has been featured on CNN, and her writing published by The Huffington Post, Elephant Journal, and Quartz.

Made in the USA
San Bernardino, CA
06 December 2019

61028848R00060